A View from My Deck

Haikus Inspired by Nature

All poetry contained in this work is the original work of the author.

Published by St. Petersburg Press

St. Petersburg, FL

www.stpetersburgpress.com

Design and composition by St. Petersburg Press and Pablo Guidi

Cover design by St. Petersburg Press and Pablo Guidi, photo by Timothy Huff

Print ISBN: 978-1-940300-20-7

eBook ISBN: 978-1-940300-21-4

First Edition

A View from My Deck

Haikus Inspired by Nature

Timothy Huff

This book is dedicated to Randy, who I had to run and get every time I found another gift.

The Spring of 2020 came with a quarantine from the corona virus. I found refuge sitting on my back deck taking in all the gifts from Mother Nature. As the days went on, I found myself studying those nature gifts closer. At the same time a friend invited everyone to join her in a daily haiku. After thinking about it for several days, I was inspired by the jasmine with the full moon behind it, on the back arbor, looking like black lace. Maybe a Stevie Nicks moment? That started my journey of simple daily haikus inspired by nature.

Thanks Sandie!

Simple Haiku

#1
Oh jasmine! Full moon!
So bright pink behind you now
New black lace on moon

#2
Dark gloomy morning
No energy from the sun
Nature continues

#3
As I step outside
What cool morning breeze delight
New spring leaves flutter

#4
Monday morning here
Search gifts from Mother Nature
Two orchid blooms here

#5

Cardinals whistle

Bodhi tree to jug to drink

Sparrows chirp, birds sing

#6
Orange and yellow
Fluttering in the warm breeze
Butterflies delight

#7
Cool breeze washes me
So sweet, jasmine fills the air
Love simple pleasures

#8
Oh angels bowling?
No, thunder is rolling in
Lightning signals strike

#9
Rain, so refreshing
Water energy needed
All plants are smiling

#10
Big fat bumble bee
Lands on delicate flower
Oh but never falls

#11
Caladium leaves pop
Red, green, pink, white swirl and mix
Color mandala

#12
As soft breezes blow
Wind chimes make their sweet music
New movement, new song

#13
Lovely gardenia
With sweet scent so heavenly
Petals pure and white

#14

Cute small brown flyers
"His eye is on the sparrow"
Sweet chirp is his song

#15
Cool rain so needed
Replenish and refresh all
Nature is smiling

#16
After the rain, toads
Join the concert at the pond
Croaking serenade

#17
Hi mister squirrel
So curious and carefree
Jesters of nature

#18
Frangipani bloom
White bloom with yellow center
Heavenly scent too

#19
Red amaryllis
So majestic and regal
Floral royalty

#20
Soft long green tendrils
Mother Nature lace so fine
The beauty of fern

#21
Delightful cool morn'
Summer warmth lies just ahead
Oh refreshing breeze

#22
Night blooming jasmine
Tiny white powerful blooms
Master of fragrance

#23
Bleeding heart so red
All butterflies adore thee
Along fence you go

#24
Lizard friend appears
Guardian of his own space
No little bugs here

#25
Pretty lantana
Your cute little bouquets
Nature's confetti

#26
Baby bird up above
Shouts I am hungry to mom
Here she comes with food

#27
See caterpillar
Making his new chrysalis
Soon a butterfly

#28
Intricate, complex
Wonderment of spider's web
Master of detail

#29

Croak here, there, tree frogs

Calling out invites to party

Gather at the pond

#30
Soft yellow canna
Sneaking up thru iris fronds
Summer pond flower

#31
Wild crazy blue jay
Your rich regal blue saves you
Troublesome yard kid

#32
Unique dragon fly
Zipping and dotting allover
Fairies chariot ride

#33
Our newest visitor
So distinguished starling bird
Black with yellow beak

#34
Little ladybug
Jazzy orange with black dots
And you can fly too

#35
Glow of morning sun
Shining thru leaves and petals
Nature's own stained glass

#36
Love Mother Nature
Daily gifts and wonderments
Oh look another one

Photography: Sheri Kendrick

Timothy Huff, a Binghamton, New York transplant, is a
lover of nature and sunshine - which brought him to our
beautiful St. Petersburg some 30+ years ago. He lives his
Florida dream with husband Randy and his dog, Toby.

A custom window treatment designer by profession, the
COVID crisis brought out his inner poet, sharing Haikus
with online friends.

Tim joyfully shares collected observations of the life he loves
with you...

CPSIA information can be obtained
at www.ICGtesting.com
Printed in the USA
LVHW041933150920
666053LV00006B/623